AF587814

Find Out what your Profile is with your phone/browser

1. Go to **www.baziprofiling.com/profile**

2. Key in your Date of Birth

3. Your Structure is instantly revealed

Your Main Profile is:

THE PERFORMER

(Hurting Officer)

* The calculator will automatically convert your Western date of birth to Chinese in deriving your Profile

傷官格

THE PERFORMER

(Hurting Officer)

BaZi Profiling: The Ten Profiles
THE PERFORMER (Hurting Officer Profile)

First Edition May 2010
2nd Print June 2011

The author can be reached at:

Mastery Academy of Chinese Metaphysics Sdn. Bhd. (611143-A)
19-3, The Boulevard, Mid Valley City,
59200 Kuala Lumpur, Malaysia.
Tel : +603-2284 8080
Fax : +603-2284 1218
Website : www.masteryacademy.com

Published by JY Books Sdn. Bhd. (659134-T)

INDEX

MASTERY ACADEMY
OF CHINESE METAPHYSICS™

At **www.masteryacademy.com**, you will find some useful tools to ascertain key information about the Feng Shui of a property or for the study of Astrology.

The Joey Yap Flying Stars Calculator can be utilised to plot your home or office Flying Stars chart. To find out your personal best directions, use the 8 Mansions Calculator. To learn more about your personal Destiny, you can use the Joey Yap BaZi Ming Pan Calculator to plot your Four Pillars of Destiny – you just need to have your date of birth (day, month, year) and time of birth.

For more information about BaZi, Xuan Kong or Flying Star Feng Shui, or if you wish to learn more about these subjects with Joey Yap, logon to the Mastery Academy of Chinese Metaphysics website at **www.masteryacademy.com.**

MASTERY ACADEMY
E-LEARNING CENTER

www.maelearning.com

Bookmark this address on your computer, and visit this newly-launched website today. With the E-Learning Center, knowledge of Chinese Metaphysics is a mere 'click' away!

Our E-Learning Center consists of 3 distinct components.

1. Online Courses
These shall comprise of 3 Programs: our Online Feng Shui Program, Online BaZi Program, and Online Mian Xiang Program. Each lesson contains a video lecture, slide presentation and downloadable course notes.

2. MA Live!
With MA Live!, Joey Yap's workshops, tutorials, courses and seminars on various Chinese Metaphysics subjects broadcasted right to your computer screen. Better still, participants will not only get to see and hear Joey talk 'live', but also get to engage themselves directly in the event and more importantly, TALK to Joey via the MA Live! interface. All the benefits of a live class, minus the hassle of actually having to attend one!

3. Video-On-Demand (VOD)
Get immediate streaming-downloads of the Mastery Academy's wide range of educational DVDs, right on your computer screen. No more shipping costs and waiting time to be incurred!

Study at your own pace, and interact with your Instructor and fellow students worldwide...at your own convenience and privacy. With our E-Learning Center, knowledge of Chinese Metaphysics is brought DIRECTLY to you in all its clarity, with illustrated presentations and comprehensive notes expediting your learning curve!

Welcome to the Mastery Academy's E-LEARNING CENTER...
YOUR virtual gateway to Chinese Metaphysics mastery!

傷官格

THE PERFORMER

(Hurting Officer)

IINTRODUCTION

Have you ever experienced dealing with someone difficult and thought, *He is so talented, but too bad he is impossible to work with,* or *She is a genius but too bad she can't get along with anyone?* It is disappointing to know that such people will never reach their full potential because they do not know their strengths and weaknesses. They don't understand others, and neither do they seem to understand themselves.

But what if that person is YOU – and you just don't know it?

Who you are determines your perception towards others. Who you are determines the angle or perspective from which you view the world. What people see is greatly influenced or perhaps even controlled by their self-image and their identity. Give it a test right now – people in the same room as you will see the exact things, issues, events, ideas and other people that you see in a totally different way.

Why?

Well, because of their unique identity – their LENS with which they view life. This LENS is the subject of the third level in my BaZi Profiling™ series of books – known as the Ten BaZi Profiles.

Your personality comes through to others when you work with others, when you talk about others, when you are in a relationship with others or perhaps when you are just interacting with others. But it takes time for us get to know people, to mingle with them and learn things that we can't learn through observation alone.

BaZi Profiles offers us the quickest way to look through the lens of others or even our own, clearly. Simply put, the only way to change how we view life is to change who we are on the inside.

Every human being has a unique BaZi Profile. This Profile represents our personal frame of reference that consists of our attitudes, assumptions and expectations concerning ourselves, other people and life. This unique set of factors determines whether we are optimistic of pessimistic, happy or sad, jovial or gloomy, trusting or suspicious, friendly or conservative, courageous or shy, patient or temperamental, logical or emotional. These factors colour how we see life as well as how we influence or are influenced by others.

The BaZi Profiles: The Roles You Play in the World

My **BaZi Profiling** series of books are based on my BaZi Personality Profiling™ System, which I've developed based on an ancient, time-tested system of Chinese Astrology known as BaZi八字. I've synthesized the entire system of BaZi into a simple and direct format that enables us to directly analyze a person's personality and behavior at three different levels, based simply on his or her date of birth. And all this is done without the need for any technical knowledge of Astrology.

Too many people are only familiar with the "12 Animal Year Signs" type of Chinese Astrology. But the true form of character traits in Chinese Astrology stems from a complex interplay of all the factors in a BaZi chart, and not just the Year of Birth. This is because in BaZi Profiling™ there is actually a combination of 500 different types of personality models!

Of course, delving into the full system of BaZi in great depth can be a tad bit daunting. That is why I've endeavored to present the system in an extremely simple, easy-to-understand format to enable general enthusiasts to immediately utilize BaZi Profiling™ to understand themselves and motivate, inspire and transform others through understanding other people's profiles.

My first two series of books:

1. The ***BaZi Profiling: 10 Day Masters***; and
2. ***BaZi Profiling: 5 Structures***;

cover the first two levels of my BaZi Profiling™ System. To get a concise and clear idea of the full picture, refer to the following chart:

10 Day Masters (Level 1)

Who You Are – The Day Master reveals your *basic character*; your essential personality traits, strengths and weaknesses fall under this.

5 Structures (Level 2)

How You Approach the World – The Structure reveals your personality *in relation* to the world. In essence, your BaZi Structure shows you your *modus operandi* – why you behave the way you do, and what attitudes you project in life.

10 Profiles (Level 3)

What You Do – The Profile reveals your individual lifestyle. It helps you understand what you do in the world, and how your actions are manifested. Your BaZi Profile explains your 'style' of operation in life. It is about the work, intimate and social masks that you wear to function as an unique individual.

The book you are holding in your hands belongs to the ***BaZi Profiling: 10 Profiles*** series, the Profiles being the third level of BaZi Profiling.

If you don't know what your BaZi chart or Profile is, don't worry. You can log on to my website at http://www.baziprofiling.com/profile to plot your chart and find out your Profile instantly.

Be Yourself, Only Better

We all know that our attitude is what MAKES or UNMAKES us. It is really not the circumstances, the bank account and the conditions of our birth that shape our life. We have complete control over our attitudes. Whether our outlook in life is positive or negative, expectant or reluctant, receptive or repulsive, open or closed is completely our choice.

I call this being at the "HEALTHY" or "UNHEALTHY" states of our BaZi Profile.

When your Profile is functioning at a healthy level, you exert a more positive attitude or reveal a more positive side of your BaZi Profile. When you are functioning at an unhealthy state, you tend to exert a more negative side of your Profile. It is important to clarify here that the level of 'healthiness' of a Profile has nothing to do with a person's actual physical health condition. "Healthy" or "Unhealthy" is a term I use to describe the states of a BaZi Profile where *healthy* means it is in a positive state and *unhealthy* means it is in a negative state.

Do take note that the Profile of every person will fluctuate between the levels of healthy and unhealthy throughout his or her life. The degree of this fluctuation depends on some extent the time, events and circumstances in life as well as influences from other people. But here's a secret – you can, BY CHOICE – choose to behave at the 'healthy' state of your Profile.

It's all about being YOU, but only BETTER.

It is amazing how two individuals of the same BaZi Profile can still be so different. This is because one may be functioning at a healthy level while the other is functioning at an unhealthy level. So make a conscious CHOICE to be better, according to your personal profile. Change is easy as you are only being yourself (but in a positive state).

The bar graph below shows the fluctuating levels of healthiness of a BaZi Profile.

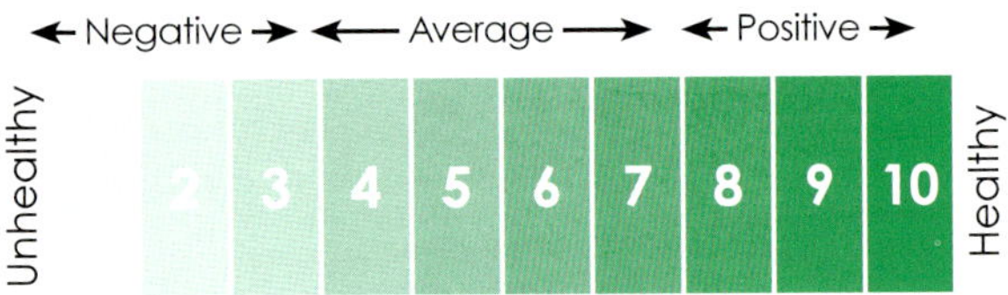

Life Transformation – Designing Your Destiny

What is it that shapes our attitudes? It's our character. And how can we change something like our character if we don't know what our character is? That's why it is essential to first begin by being aware of your PROFILE.

I'm sure you've met or even known people who are their own 'worst enemy.' They always, for some reason, manage to sabotage themselves when success (in the form of a relationship or a dream job, for example) is just within reach.

Who we are – our self-image – can restrict or expand our ability to achieve success in life. A person with an unhealthy self-image or at what I call the "unhealthy levels of their BaZi Profile" will not achieve sustainable success in life because he will eventually bring himself down to the level of his own innate expectations as permissible by the 'health level' of his Profile.

Isn't it strange that human nature seems to endow all of us with the natural ability and instincts to size up or judge everyone else on earth except for ourselves?

Many people know that for things to change, they first need to change themselves. But how can they change, when they don't know WHAT to change? That is why all change – begins with SELF-AWARENESS.

This means the person they need to first get to know is YOURSELF. Many experts on relationship will say – you've got to be your own best friend first in order to improve yourself and have better relationships with others. True. But how do you 'become best friends' with someone you don't now or you don't even like? You simply can't!

Hence the purpose of BaZi Profiles is to help you understand YOURSELF.

If we ask ourselves (honestly) to give a kick in the butt to that ONE person who got us into all our troubles and emotional pain in life, I think we will find ourselves rather sore by now.

Take a look around: the people who often complain about difficulties in work or in relationships are often looking at everyone else but themselves to explain the problem.

With AWARENESS of ourselves – we understand and clearly see WHO we are. When we understand who we are we can come to the next stage – and that's REALIZATION.

We will begin to realize that the true source many of our problems are ourselves. We are the problem. Our mentalities, expectations, reservations, attitudes and habits form the biggest challenges and obstacles to our own success!

BaZi Profiling describes accurately our inner motives and habitual responses that greatly influence our individual character and molds and shapes our destiny. It allows us to diagnose how we function on the inside, and how we present ourselves on the outside.

Knowing What to Do... and Doing It

Everything you've ever experienced, good or bad is attributed to who you are. Your Profile is your lens to the outside world.

The printout of your Profile chart from my website, as mentioned earlier, will indicate clearly your Main Profile as well as its complementary side – that is, your Sub Profile (or Secondary Profile).

The Main Profile shows your primary role in life while your Sub Profile tells you your secondary role. Both profiles are equally important as human beings are complex creatures. We play different roles in different circumstances and environments in life. Who we are at work can be totally different from who we are at home.

In this book, you will also see sections describing your **Intimate Subtype** and **Social Subtype**.

Intimate Subtype describes your relationship mask - how you respond, react and behave in a relationship. Your Social Subtype describes your social mask – how you behave with close friends and in the world at large.

There is also a section describing your Hidden Nature. A person's hidden nature relates to what is on the inside. What subtly drives and motivates you to do the things you do and behave the way you do? Some of these hidden attributes may be aspects or traits that you aren't even consciously aware of.

You will also discover how your Profile operates in your career, and while under pressure. Learn the types of jobs that are easiest for your Profile to pursue. Discover what kinds of industries or disciplines towards which you're naturally inclined. And more importantly, learn how to become more effective in your work. To do this we will also discuss your profile's leadership style and what kind of skills will need to acquire to enable you to become more influential as a leader.

One Profile Fits All?

Human beings are multifaceted and complex. It is impossible that any one person has only ONE Profile that defines their entire life. Most people have multiple roles, and hence will the need to know the Main, Secondary, Social and Intimate profiles.

You do also need to bear in mind that this book shows you the traits of a Profile *in general*, and doesn't take into account the particularities of your entire BaZi chart.

If you find that you are living your life at the "unhealthy" state of your BaZi Profile, you will need to take conscious steps to initiate a change. This book may be used as a guide.

However if the DIY method is not effective enough for you, I will recommend that you engage one of my BaZi Personality Profiling ™ life coaches to help you. A one-on-one coaching session will do two things: 1. Help you better understand your Profile; and 2. Help you plan a course of action to make a transformation for the better. Let us help you maximize the strengths of YOUR profile so that you can be a better you.

And perhaps if you'd like to take this subject further and help others – I would suggest taking one of my BaZi Profiling™ workshops that are offered around the world. Learn how to decode BaZi Profiles and solve PEOPLE problems. I call this PEOPLE-knowledge. Or perhaps you simply want to know more about people so that you could choose friends wisely and manage employees better. Attending one of our live workshops would serve any one of these purposes.

BaZi Profiling™ is a study that is designed to helps us understand ourselves better and make informed decisions, and ultimately, enables us to shape our life for the better.

Your best investment in life is yourself. Once you activate the strengths of your BaZi Profile, you will begin to walk on the Path of Least Resistance to Success!

Joey Yap
June 2010

 www.facebook.com/joeyyapFB

Author's personal website :
www.joeyyap.com

Academy websites :
www.masteryacademy.com l www.maelearning.com l www.baziprofiling.com

Three Levels of BaZi Profiling

In BaZi Profiling, there are three levels that reflect three different stages of a person's personal nature and character structure.

Level 1 – The Day Master

The Day Master in a nutshell is the BASIC YOU. The inborn personality. It is your essential character. It answers the basic question "WHO AM I". There are ten basic personality profiles – the TEN Day Masters – each with its unique set of personality traits, likes and dislikes.

Level 2 – The Structure

The Structure is your behavior and attitude – in other words, how you use your personality. It expands on the Day Master (Level 1). The structure reveals your natural tendencies in life – are you more controlling, more of a creator, supporter, thinker or connector? Each of the Ten Day Masters express themselves differently through the FIVE Structures. Why do we do the things we do? Why do we like the things we like? – The answers are in our BaZi STRUCTURE.

Level 3 – The Profile

YOU ARE HERE

The Profile reveals your unique abilities and skills, the masks that you consciously and unconsciously "put on" as you approach and navigate the world. Your Profile speaks of your ROLES in life. There are TEN roles – or Ten BaZi Profiles. Everyone plays a different role.

What makes you happy and what does success mean to you is different to somebody else. Your sense of achievement and sense of purpose in life is unique to your Profile. Your Profile will reveal your unique style.

The path of least resistence to your success and wealth can only be accessed once you get into your "flow." Your BaZi Profile reveals how you can get FLOW. It will show you your patterns in work, relationship and social settings. Being AWARE of these patterns is your first step to positive Life Transformation.

www.baziprofiling.com

傷官格

THE PERFORMER

(Hurting Officer)

INTRODUCTION

The Hurting Officer Structure (傷官) in BaZi is known as the Performer Profile. As its name suggests, the Performer Profile is all about being the star of any show. Performer Profiles are creative, ambitious, highly-driven, and success and image-oriented folks. They pursue perfection and are extremely driven. Performer Profiles are usually fast learners and are typically rather street-smart.

Performer Profiles like to put their best foot forward at all times, be it intellectually, creatively, or physically – and hence, are extremely polished and sophisticated. They are very competent and adaptable, and are more often than not ready to take on a challenge. They are imbued with an active sense of energy, and constantly strive to improve themselves.

From the start, Performer Profiles have their eye on the goal. They love success, and they adore glamour. On the flipside, they're also terribly afraid of failure, and of being insignificant. This means that they can sometimes be shallow, vain, and unpredictable. They have too many interests, and may sometimes spread themselves too thin. Performer Profiles have strong opinions and can sometimes be perceived as being argumentative and highly critical.

The 10 Profiles can be divided into two groups: Yin, and Yang. The Performer Profile falls under Yang. Indeed, it may seem like the Performer Profile invented the category of the Yang! They love the limelight, and are completely at ease in it. Their personal magnetism is their own greatest brand, and their greatest value.

Their "pull" factors - Performer Profiles are motivated by:

- The need to feel valuable and worthwhile
- Being effective and efficient
- Being able to perform well
- Being the best
- The ability to excel and to be affirmed in excellence
- The need to be admired, and to impress others

Their "push" factors – Performer Profiles are demotivated by:

- Looking like a "failure"
- Sitting around doing nothing
- Being overshadowed by others
- Being caught unprepared
- Having to ask for help
- Coming off as simply average

Recognizing the Performer Profile

Personality

Creative

Unusual solutions from unique minds

Performer Profiles are invested in their own personalities and how they present themselves to the world. They're not willing or keen to be a dime a dozen. They need to stand out in a crowd, and make themselves count. For this, they use their creativity to help them be branded as special, distinctive, different. In fact, the Performer Profile would be nothing without its unique way of thinking.

Therefore, their creativity is often a hallmark of an inquisitive mind. Performer Profiles like to know about things and investigate their origins and mechanisms. Doing so helps them think about things differently than the average person. They are extremely flexible and allow for all sorts of internal shifts of viewpoints. Thus, they're rarely the types who think of the same stale thing everyone has already thought about twice.

Their creativity and original sense of vision makes them much-desired in the workplace, and in personal relationships. Performer Profiles are rarely bored with the world, and consequently, people who spend time with Performer Profiles are rarely ever bored with them! This makes them interesting, entertaining people to be with – which goes a long way to explain their success with people, and their popularity in general.

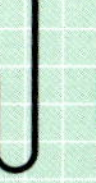

KEY TRAITS

- **Unique-thinking**
- **Non-conformist mindset**
- **Original vision**
- **Flexible perspectives**

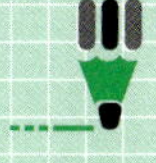

Charismatic

Having the power of allure

It doesn't take much effort for healthy Performer Profiles to grab the attention of others, or hold people in thrall. They usually have a certain something – a certain intangible quality – that makes others sort of flock to them. Like a light that attracts the moths, Performer Profiles are able to command a roomful of strangers in a party to stand around them as they pontificate on some theory or another, or be able to achieve some measure of fame if they're public figures.

They're charisma derives in large part from their investment and involvement in their image and persona. Performer Profile folks consider their image to be a very important extension of themselves, and therefore spend a lot of time cultivating it. This marks them out in a crowd of people who don't really think too much about the impressions they present. Performer Profiles are smart about putting their best foot forward.

Performer Profiles are also imbued with a sort of infectious and energy that draws people to them. Because they often want to excel and be the best of whatever they do, they make an effort to be admired. They strive to be presentable and appropriate, and don't want to come across in ways that might be disapproved of by others. Despite their apparent air of untouchability or superiority, Performer Profiles need the approval and response of other people.

KEY TRAITS

- **Possess appeal to others**
- **Have intrinsic allure**
- **Polished image**
- **Want to be admired**

Ambitious
Aiming for the top

Performer Profiles are, above and beyond, goal-oriented. Once they have a particular objective in their sight, they actively engage in activities and measures that will bring them closer to that particular goal. Performer Profiles don't sit around waiting to be feted by good luck – they go out there and make their own luck. They pursue their dreams tirelessly, and cannot understand why others are not similarly motivated and enthusiastic.

Thus, they are extremely organised and very competent. They are also effective in the sense that they align their actions with their objectives; they don't believe in the "wait and see" mode of being. As such, healthy Performer Profiles are not afraid of hard work. They don't see hard work as a sacrifice; instead they simply see it as necessary. Or even if viewed as some form of sacrifice, it's a necessary sacrifice, and there's no use whining about it – just get to work!

Healthy Performer Profiles like helping others become that way, too – to help others mine for their own ambitions and goals and set forth on a plan to achieve them. Therefore, they enjoy sharing self-development tips, explanations on how to make money, lose weight, develop career skills, and others along that nature. They are very results-oriented.

KEY TRAITS

- Desire to excel
- Results-oriented
- Hardworking and efficient
- Pursue dreams tirelessly

Arrogant

Better than everyone else

When Performer Profiles are unhealthy or operating on a level that's not their best, they can become very arrogant and suffer from delusions of grandeur. They start to think that only they can achieve the best, and only they know the way to achieve the best – regardless of whether or not this is true. The "trueness" of their success is sometimes not evident to themselves.

This is because they can easily fool themselves into thinking that they're operating on the plane of excellence at all times. Sometimes, they reject forms of success that are different from what they think they're meant to have. For example, they may on occasion reject the runner-up award for not having won the main prize, and may find ways to disparage the real winner.

To that extent, Performer Profiles may also exaggerate their own abilities and strengths. This kind of self-deception can cause the Performer Profile a great deal of suffering, not to mention alienate them from the people around them. In some unhealthy Performer Profiles, once they lose themselves in their arrogance, they keep going without any remorse because they're unable to see the difference – or simply refuse to see it.

KEY TRAITS

- Grandiose about own accomplishments
- Scoffs at others
- May be self-deceitful
- Exaggerate own abilities

Aggressive
Taking competition too far

Performer Profiles who are operating on an unfavourable level can take their healthy ambition a little too far. Competitiveness becomes their default mode of being, and everything becomes a contest. Something as simple as a person suggesting a different route to get to restaurant may be viewed as an affront to their own suggestions, and they'll try to find ways to make the other suggestion fail, or compare it endlessly.

This need to compete for everything makes the Performer Profile a very aggressive, intense personality – and more than a little bit difficult to deal with. When they become excessively driven, they forget everything else but the final goal or destination, and will cast aside any reservations about the methods they employ in order to get there.

As expected, the casualties of this kind of take-no-prisoners type drive for excellence are other people. There is really no excuse for pushing people to the wayside in the quest for excellence – unless those people are genuinely preventing you from achieving success by behaving badly. Otherwise, unhealthy Performer Profiles who operate on this level will suffer from intense loneliness and alienation.

KEY TRAITS

- Too forceful in competition
- Critical of everything
- Compares self to everyone else
- Inadvertently exacerbating own loneliness

Hidden Nature

The section on Hidden Nature highlights the private traits of each Profile, traits that are not made easily visible to the external world. In some cases, these traits will continue to lie submerged in the Profile's psyche, known only to the people themselves, or is only revealed to those who are closest to them. Alternatively, these traits may be unconsciously revealed to others in particular moments.

It is called "hidden" because it's the sub-conscious behaviour that apparently they themselves are not aware of, and others may only have a glimpse of this after knowing them for a long time as it is concealed and out of immediate sight. The hidden self is typically the driving force of their behaviour.

Self-doubting
Never good enough

Underneath their self-aggrandizing facade, Performer Profiles have deep-rooted anxieties about their personal value. They often have the irrational fear that they may not be quite "good enough", despite any evidence to the contrary. Therefore, they are always beating themselves up for not having done enough or achieved enough. There's always this invisible bar of excellence that seems out of their reach.

Performer Profiles thus have to keep pushing themselves in order to feel some sort of inner worth. Therefore, it becomes quite difficult after awhile to tell if the Performer Profile is truly working towards a legitimate goal, or is simply on auto-pilot chasing after pipe dreams that may not have any bearing or relevance to their actual goals.

Performer Profiles desperately want to be affirmed and valued, but they place too much priority on the externals. Going by their strong nature, it would seem that they would be able to heed their inner voice and gauge their own self-worth. However, the opposite is the case. Above and beyond, their self-doubt arises because their foundations are built on shaky externals.

KEY TRAITS

- Deep anxieties about personal value
- Feeling never good enough
- Always something more to achieve
- Fear of never being able to achieve "right" form of success

Highly-pressured

Under great stress to maintain reputation

Performer Profiles are under great internal pressure to live up to the high expectations they think others have of them. Although, in truth, these high expectations are of their own creation. Other folks don't nearly judge them as harshly as they do themselves. In that sense, they can be said to be their own worst enemy.

People of the Performer Profile feel that unless they maintain a certain position or image in life, they will be devalued and rejected, and tossed aside as worthless. They never want to look like they're being overshadowed by others, or be caught unprepared or unawares. Most of all, they never want to be thought of as average, or just a regular person.

Therefore, they push themselves hard – sometimes too hard. They feel that unless they "keep it together", they will be unmasked for a fraud. This means that they're internal voice is one of constant comparison – and by extension, criticism. Performer Profiles feel like they always have to be "on" and on-edge to ensure they slip off the cliff into an abyss of irrelevance, or worse still, normalcy and blandness.

KEY TRAITS

- High expectations of themselves
- Constantly need to maintain reputation
- Afraid of being devalued or rejected
- Tie their self-worth to being special

Volatile

Up one day, down the next

Another interesting aspect of the Performer Profile's hidden nature is their inner volatility. This is intriguing because their external reputation is based on measured uncertainty. Their reputation counts on the fact that they're exciting, hence they're never predictable or boring. However, there is always some form of control to the amount of changeability they portray to the world.

On the inside, however, Performer Profiles are able to swing from one extreme to another in terms of self-evaluation and emotions. This is because they derive their sense of self from external cues most of the time. When the public opinion is good, then they're on top of the world. When the tide changes, however, they can dip into low spirits and internal depression.

This is not shown to everyone, of course, because the Performer Profile is not keen to share its vulnerabilities to the world. They may occasionally feel empty and emotionally-isolated, and may purposely stay away from others or keep people at bay. Someone who was once the life of the party will now just want to hole up in their room and be left alone.

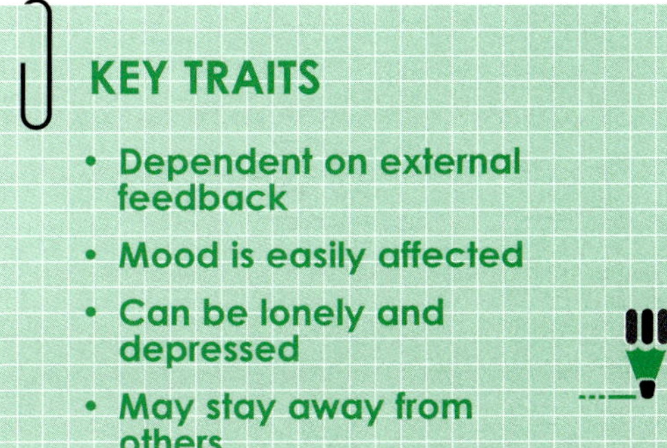

KEY TRAITS

- Dependent on external feedback
- Mood is easily affected
- Can be lonely and depressed
- May stay away from others

Performer Profile Dynamics and Variations

In BaZi, the Profile is only one aspect of what is a very complex study. There are other concepts to take into consideration as a whole, such as the Day Master and the Structure, and more importantly, the strength of the elements that form the Day Master, the Structure, and the Profile.

The concept of strong or weak elements is a fundamental aspect of BaZi, and plays a big role in determining whether a particular Profile is healthy or unhealthy. The strength and quality of your Profile, or its level of health, are based upon the factors that are inherent in your individual BaZi chart.

The Profile Under Pressure reveals how a person belonging to the Profile is likely to behave in situations that are stressful or nerve-wracking, or around other people who create a taxing atmosphere.

The Positive Side
(Healthy Level)

- **Focused**

Whatever Performer Profile wants, Performer Profile gets. Capable, efficient, ad ready to do the work, Performer Profile people set objectives and do whatever is in their power to achieve them. Others can take a page out of Performer Profile's style and learn how to work for what they want in order to get measurable results. Performer Profiles consider free time and blank slates as opportunities, and use it to focus on getting what they want.

- **Confident**

Performer Profiles require a lot of courage to go about their business, and the healthy ones are typically very confident and assured. Hence, the image they project and the person they are on the inside are not contradictions. They know what they're capable of, and strive for the best because they think that they deserve it. Healthy Performer Profiles are also eager to help others to do the same.

• **Genuine**

When they're at their best, Performer Profile people are authentic in their aims in life. That's when what they project on the outside is in synchronicity with what is inside. Then, their goals are actually their own, and they have no uncertainty or insecurity about achieving them – as opposed to less healthy Performer Profiles who chase for success as defined by others' terms.

- **Articulate**

Part of the Performer Profile's appeal is their ability to express themselves. They are often sharp and witty in conversation, and infuse their speech with an undercurrent of dry yet easily-relatable humour. Also, they are extremely articulate, and speak clearly and with purpose, and have no problems conveying exactly what they mean. Lots of healthy Performer Profiles are able public speakers.

- **Competent**

Performer Profiles are extremely fast-learners, and can pick up new skills very swiftly. As a result, they are often very competent regardless of which end of the water they're thrown into. Blending their keen intelligence with a strong sense of street-smarts, Performer Profiles rarely feel like they're in over their heads and this knowledge of their own competence enables them to set high goals.

- **Energetic**

One of the most endearing things about Performer Profiles is their high-level of energy they bring to anything that they do. These are not wilting flowers who do things half-heartedly; one foot in and the other foot out. They are able to inspire and motivate other people through this display of infectious verve and enthusiastic energy.

The Negative Side
(Unhealthy Level)

- **Boastful**

When unfavourable, Performer Profiles can almost appear like toddlers in their bid to boast about their impressive achievements (whether real or imagined). They can appear extremely boastful, which presents a negative impression of them as somehow immature and vain in some way. In their unhealthy moments, Performer Profiles can come off as being extremely self-involved to the point of narcissism.

- **Overbearing**

At their worst, Performer Profiles are very intense and overbearing, and can tend to be rather forceful. Others might feel somehow stifled or suffocated in the presence of a Performer Profile person. Again, this is due to their inflated sense of self-importance, where they start to believe that their words and actions are the only "correct" ones, or that they're the only ones who will save the day.

- **Selfish**

The less favourable the Performer Profile, the more selfish they become. They stop caring or taking interest in the needs and interests of other people, and no longer see the need to help other people achieve their goals. It becomes a classic case of "me" syndrome, where their own desires trump all others. This is closely linked to the unhealthy Performer Profile's self-obsession and sense of grandiosity.

- **Belligerent**

At their best, Performer Profiles are rarely retiring wallflowers or people who keep their true opinions to themselves. They are usually quite verbal and will share their perspective on matters. But in the negative sense, they can become quite argumentative and outright belligerent, and can even be rather aggressive in manner if people don't agree with them.

• **Shallow**

Performer Profiles care very much about their image and reputation. Sometimes, they can become too addicted about putting only the "right" foot forward. It may seem like a catastrophe if the wrong foot is presented, instead. As such, they can become too obsessed with all the shallow, external trappings of glitz, glamour, and reputation that they neglect their inner fundamentals.

- **Critical**

Once they start to believe that their own view of things is best, Performer Profiles can become extremely critical towards themselves, and in extension, to others as well. They can be incredibly interfering in the lives of others, and may offer unwarranted "advice" that sound more like orders of what to do. If their opinions aren't taken, they can become extremely negative and condescending, passing off judgments on what others are doing.

The Performer Profile Under Pressure

- **Routine**

When the Performer Profile is under stress, he or she tends to go into autopilot. Their stress is magnified and beyond what they can cope with, and they tend to shut down and take solace in routine because it doesn't tax their mental faculties.

- **Lose focus**

Or, alternatively, they may go into autopilot in terms of being busy, and occupy themselves with needless activities. Or they may simply be doing things to give off the appearance that they're getting things done when they're actually unable to cope.

- **Depressed**

When the stress becomes too much, they begin to shut down and become listless and their trademark energy is snuffed out. They may become depressed and feel hopeless. They will want others to leave them alone and give them space.

- **Resistant to help**

In vein of shutting down and becoming listless, they also start refusing help – and become very adamant about not taking help from the others. They will shove away all offers of assistance.

Intimate Performer Profile

The Self with Others

The Intimate Subtype and What It Means

In BaZi Profiling, the Profile can be divided into two subtypes, the Intimate Subtype and the Social Subtype.

The Intimate Subtype essentially refers to the growing awareness of the self with an "other" – i.e. another person. It starts out in life with the Profile's parents or primary caregivers, and then as the person grows up and starts taking his or her place in the world, with one's close friends, partners, and/or spouse.

This section typically emphasises how the Profile engages with the intimate other, and the psychological thinking and behaviour that may motivate or give impulse to their actions and words. The Intimate Subtype reflects how the person of this Profile behaves when in a relationship, or looking for one. It refers to their relationship mask.

Charming

Possessing attractive appeal

In their relationships within the romantic sphere, Performer Profiles are very invested in what it means to be traditionally attractive from a masculine or feminine viewpoint. Thus, they ensure that they are always pleasant and appealing to the people whom they want to attract. They make concentrated efforts to be perceived as such.

Performer Profiles therefore have strong charm that works on other people and makes others find them very attractive. Establishing relationships is not a very difficult job for the Performer Profile. In fact, it almost comes as a second nature! They know exactly how to behave in order to get the attention of others.

Furthermore, Performer Profiles are gifted with the silver tongue, and know how to make sweet speech sound even sweeter. This, combined with their quick wit and intelligence, often makes them highly desirable partners and companions. They are able to highlight all the high points in their partners and draw out the best, and can be very diplomatic and accommodating if they choose to be.

KEY TRAITS

- **Witty and intelligent**
- **Appealing in looks**
- **Attractive in speech**
- **Knows how to compliment people**

Exciting

Never a dull moment

Performer Profiles thrive on some form of excitement, as this is what fuels their energy. They detest predictable routines, because what is there to talk about if one is doing the same thing day after day? As such, they often like to experience a new thing every so often, and try to be on their toes in order to fit in as much as they can into a given day.

In their relationships and friendships, therefore, Performer Profiles bring an aura of excitement to the proceedings. They are always sought-after guests at dinner parties and events, because they will be sure to keep others rapt with their sparkling conversation and risqué (only within boundaries) opinions. It's hard to fall asleep during the dessert course if one is seated next to the Performer Profile!

As befits their name, too, Performer Profiles like to entertain. They are quite attuned to the barometer of public perception (because they want to be admired and liked) and so will be ready to be flexible and switch things up if they sense that the people whom they're with are starting to become bored, restless, or listless. In this sense, Performer Profile folks are always 100% "on".

KEY TRAITS

- Thrives on excitement
- Doesn't like to be bored
- Doesn't like to bore others
- Flexible and ready to adapt

Remote

Using busyness as a barrier

When in a negative state, Performer Profiles suffer from a fear of intimacy. They are afraid of being rejected, or being thought of as not good enough. Therefore, they're highly-capable minds go into overdrive in order to prevent this from happening. Typically, Performer Profiles tend to throw themselves into their work – their personal or professional goals – to detract from any intimacy issues.

Therefore, they are very likely to use their workaholism as a way to avoid dealing with their ties to others. They may shield themselves off by getting involved in projects that are of no interests to their partner or friends, and start to miss out on meals together, or bail out of potential bonding activities. Through it all, they will make others feel silly for asking by using "I'm busy, it's work" as a crutch and an excuse.

Performer Profile folks also wall off themselves by not asking for help, and refusing to ask for help. If help is given, they may scoff at it and reject it, ensuring that it will not be offered again. They maintain an air of impenetrable distance that may exhaust anyone else who is attempting to break through it. This way, they use their remoteness as a means of avoiding true closeness.

KEY TRAITS

- Throws self into work
- Becomes a workaholic to avoid intimacy
- Projects a distant, remote air
- Will refuse offers of help

Argumentative
Picking a fight for the sake of it

Most of the time, when they're unhealthy, Performer Profiles become extremely belligerent and start to pick fights over anything at all. If they feel that a relationship has become too boring, they may use arguments as a means of adding more "excitement" to it. More often than not, they're simply asserting themselves strongly because they believe they can.

Often, this desire to enter into a dispute comes from their belief that what they belief is right, and that the other person is usually wrong (due to the fact that the Performer Profile person believes himself to be superior). Then, they may resort to uttering cutting remarks and being extremely critical about someone else's opinion, and get into arguments because of it.

At other times, Performer Profiles may start arguments with their partners (and this is particular in the case of romantic relationships) because they want to harangue the partner for not reflecting well on them. They believe they have an image to project, and it's up to their partners to fit into the scheme of things and complement the Performer Profile image. Thus, disputes and bitter fights can arise out of this misguided notion.

KEY TRAITS

- Believes opinion to be superior to others
- Berate partner for "interfering" with self-image
- Criticises others' opinions for being inferior
- May use arguments as a way of creating excitement

Social Performer Profile

The Self in the World

The Social Subtype and What It Means

In BaZi Profiling, the Profile can be divided into two subtypes, the Intimate Subtype and the Social Subtype.

The Social Subtype essentially refers to the self in interaction with the larger community of family, and extended group of friends and acquaintances, and the world at large. This will include its interactions with schoolmates, university peers, and at work, the colleagues as well as the superiors and subordinates.

The Social Subtype essentially asserts the Profile's right to belong in the world; and quite naturally, different Profiles operate in different ways in order to assert this need, and gauge its sense of place in the grander scheme of things. The Social Subtype provides hints on how the Profile may approach social causes and interact with issues and events that affect the surrounding community.

Curious

Interested in the world

One of the reasons why Performer Profiles do so well in the world at large is because they're curious about it. They have a healthy sense of inquisitiveness that displays itself admirably in the healthy Performer Profile person. Often times, they always want to know more about the people with whom they work or engage with on a daily basis – such as their neighbours, community members, and the like.

At their best, they can be very gracious and diplomatic, and ready to accept others for who they are. They do this by drawing people out and getting them to tell their stories. The healthiest Performer Profiles use their sensitivity to public perception by being engaged listeners and communicators – and their sense of wit and sharp intelligence helps them out here!

Performer Profiles are also very up-to-date on current events and what's going on in their immediate local community, and in the world at large. Staying on top of news is essential to them, and intelligent Performer Profiles are also very politicised and aware. This makes them interesting conversationalists, as they usually use these topics as a springboard for discussions with others – be it strangers they just met, or their friends.

KEY TRAITS

- Enquiring about others
- Keen to know more about people
- Very aware of events
- Keeps up with the news

Efficient

Busy with a sense of purpose

Performer Profiles are efficient, and at their best, their efficiency is not just a facade to impress others – it gets the work done. They have the highest respect for goals and proper organisation of priorities. They value effectiveness, and are especially full of admiration for people who seem capable and resourceful. They do their best to cultivate these attributes in themselves.

As such, Performer Profiles are often prized by businesses and corporations for these values. They are goal-driven; it's just an intrinsic part of their nature. When given a problem, regardless of how complex, they break it down to its respective objectives and set about targeting each one. They don't understand why others may procrastinate or self-sabotage themselves in their attempt to reach goals.

Performer Profile folks are also very reform-driven, and they can't sit by without attempting to teach an old dog new tricks. If something can be fixed and made better – they go all out to do it. Their creativity and innovation often makes them stand out, and their willingness to do the hard work gets them the kudos. They like to look at the big picture and imagine how it could if everything fell together perfectly.

KEY TRAITS

- Reform-driven
- Big-picture person
- Values effectiveness and effort
- Willing to put in the hard work to improve

Inauthentic

Confusing their goals with those of others

In the case of unhealthy Performer Profiles, inauthenticity and deceit become a part of how they operate in the world. These qualities are not something they set out to do. In fact, unhealthy Performer Profiles will be shocked to learn this about themselves. Yet, these are the qualities they inadvertently project when they start to lose touch with themselves and start identifying their needs through external cues.

Largely, the root of this is self-deception. When unhealthy, Performer Profiles may subconsciously feel that their own natural inner qualities are inadequate or unacceptable, so they strive to become the kind of person that others would look up to. They have an idea of what these qualities and talents are, and they work tirelessly to embody those qualities.

The problem is, they don't know if these are the qualities they want, or are passionate about cultivating. They may try so hard to fit into societal norms that they do not realise anymore what it is they are. Or if they do, they've long suppressed the knowledge. As a result, sometimes the unhealthy Performer Profile is like a smooth, polished shell – beautiful and shiny on the outside, but hollow and empty on the inside.

KEY TRAITS

- Prone to self-deception
- Too invested in societal norms
- Out of touch with own passions and needs
- Tireless embodying the 'ideal' figure

Status-seekers

"Love me for what I do"

At their unhealthiest, Performer Profiles can be the worst kind of social climbers and status-seekers. They might believe that they can fake it till they make it, but as time goes on, they start to lose sight of what's fake and what's real. Too often, they need to know what they're really made of by seeing what's mirrored back to them as reflected from society – but as the rest of us know, this is never an accurate gauge.

In unhealthy Performer Profiles, they may drop names like they're a phone book. They constantly quote prices, see what's most important, and focus obsessively on how much money their acquaintances have. They may start to actively seek out people who fit their idea of a glamorous or rich or successful personality. They may drop friends who don't fit this idea.

The thought of where they themselves fit on the social ladder becomes an excruciating reality to them. Much of their actions are motivated by trying to do the right thing – which might mean that they could end up cultivating friends whom they don't much like (but who are from the "right" crowd), or work at jobs they hate (but which signals the "right" kind of career progress). This type of unhealthy Performer Profile is often an unhappy one.

KEY TRAITS

- Wants the best
- Aspires to belong to the cream of society
- Makes decisions based on status
- Sacrifices personal happiness for status gains

Career Path

The Performer Profile Work Style

• Coming up with ideas

At work, the Performer Profile generally does not follow the ideas of others – it's the one that creates the ideas. They see themselves as creative, and hence creators, and prefer working out the concepts themselves. They love nothing best than to be given a blank slate and run free with their thoughts. They often view things from an aerial perspective, and are constantly thinking of how to do things from the big picture outlook. They like to keep progressing and improving, hence they always think up ways to do this.

• **Working hard**

The Performer Profile is no slouch at the work place, and they're ready to jump in with both feet. The only thing that irritates them is a lack of objectives – which, if there are none, they will simply create themselves. It's not in their nature to sit back and be lazy. They know that effort and toil are the ways in which to get someplace better than the place they're at right now.

• **Delivering results**

The busy-bee Performer Profile worker is highly valued in the workplace because he or she is committed to bringing in results. They don't toil away at the same thing if it's not giving them the outcome that they want or is expected. Therefore, they're able to be quite adaptive and proactive in switching their methods around in order to get those measurable results.

• **Being the star**

The 'performer' aspect of the Performer Profile comes into play no matter what they do – even if they're working in a relatively conservative environment, like banking. This doesn't mean that they stand on the tables and dance; it just means that they know how to attract attention to themselves. Consciously or unconsciously, they attract attention simply because it is the nature of their Profile. Smart Performer Profiles are very adept at marking themselves out as the person to watch. Usually, they tend to grab the limelight during meetings and events.

• Energising others

Performer Profiles have a high level of energy, and when they enter into a room the energy palpably changes. It could feel like they move around like a whirlwind, or there is just an extra sense of buzz and excitement in the air. However they do it, they tend to motivate others by their energetic and upbeat work style. It's hard to feel bored or lazy when working together with the Performer Profile.

- **Inspiring others**

Performer Profiles are often good at inspiring or influencing others, and they largely like to be seen as such. They are good at motivating others or rallying others around a common cause and goal, usually through their expressive and articulate sense of speech.

活力

Energy

Suitable Careers

As the Performer Profile belongs to the Yang category, they thrive in careers or industries that are somewhat glamorous or fast-paced. Their role under the limelight should preferably be witnessed by as many people as possible. They are not keen to work for tiny companies or start-ups, or if they do, there must be an opportunity to present themselves as the cream of the crop.

Please note that the suggestions below are not exhaustive, but provide a guide as to the kinds of careers in which you're likely to thrive.

PERFORMING ARTS, ENTERTAINMENT

Performer Profiles should ideally do what they do best – that is, perform. They enjoy all the extras that come with work on the stage or under the spotlight – fame, fans, and non-stop image-monitoring. They also contribute their own ideas and enjoy the freedom that comes with being largely independent, and like to selling and branding themselves as an extension of their talent.

Performer Profiles do well as artists, singers, actors, or in roles like broadcast hosts, public speakers, and talk show hosts. They are able to sway public opinion and hold an audience rapt and in thrall. The idea of their name in shining lights spurs them on to do the hard, often unglamorous work that is required to get them there.

BRANDING, MARKETING

Performer Profiles are stellar brand-developers – be it for themselves, or for another corporation. Depending on the intensity of their Hurting Officer star, certain Performer Profiles are comfortable being the face of their company by being the branding guru – they don't necessarily have to be the brand itself. Their quick-thinking, adaptive, and efficient work-style is highly-suited to this particular type of career.

As marketers, they are able to conceptualise and strategise. This is where they get to exercise their creative muscles. The challenge of reforming or improving something does not deter them – in fact, it proves to be their motivation.

MOTIVATIONAL SPEAKER, SELF-IMPROVEMENT

The self-improvement industry is a thriving one these days, and Performer Profiles are ideally suited to this job. They have the power of the spoken word, and are articulate, confident, and extremely persuasive on the job. Furthermore, they are able to use their charisma to persuade audiences and to sell a good story or a concept.

Performer Profiles who are healthy also genuinely enjoy sharing their tips with other people. As educators, they will go all out to help other people discover their potential and get started on the path of success. Because they constantly strive to be the best, it's only natural that they teach others how to do so, as well!

DESIGNERS - FASHION, INTERIOR

Performer Profiles are generally flamboyant personalities, and there is rarely a disconnect between who they are and the persona they project onto the world. As such, their creativity is fully expressed in the design industry – particularly fashion, interior, or architecture – where they can give a practical realisation to the unique concepts and ideas in their head.

Performer Profiles are also very good at branding themselves and their product, because their brand is consistent with their personality. Their creative designs are usually an expression of their innermost interests and passions, which makes it easy for them to blend personality and creativity into one package.

DESIGN

Suitable Job Roles

Regardless of the industry they decide to enter, Performer Profiles are naturally more comfortable, and a lot happier, doing certain types of jobs than others. Being in the backroom or having limited influence and exposure to the public is a sure-fire recipe for depression. They could never fully enjoy a desk-bound job that requires minimal conversation and engagement with other people. Here are some suggestions as what type of roles or positions they should play for greater satisfaction:

SKILLED PROFESSIONALS

Performer Profiles don't quite enjoy marching to the beat of another drummer. Thus, they're happiest when they're branding and selling their own skills – whatever it may be. It could be writing, acting, singing, or some other form of non-artistic skill – like lawyers, doctors. They can still be a star in their field, but they must be able to project their talents outward and call the shots.

CONSULTANTS

For Performer Profiles, the type of consulting work they like best is the kind that allows them to get up on stage on a podium, and speak to a roomful of people. Therefore, Performer Profiles enjoy work that gets them to be under a limelight and offer advice to people – especially since they tend to think that their own advice is always best! They enjoy the flexibility, freedom, and mental powers required to juxtapose user-friendly speech with technical or more intellectually-intricate theories and concepts.

EDUCATORS

What better thing to do for the Performer Profile then to address a whole bunch of people at once, and TELL them what to do? They make very entertaining and engaging teachers, especially if they're surrounded by smart, intellectually-engaged students. A healthy Performer Profile will make the best kind of teacher – lively, interesting, efficient, and able to deliver results – regardless of whether they do it in traditional schools or in different industries and educational academies and institutions.

Improving Performer Profile Effectiveness

Performer Profiles can increase their effectiveness in a number of ways that best harness their strengths and limit their weaknesses. Here are some ideas on how to do that:

1) Creatively strategise

Performer Profiles will thrive when they're able to dream up concepts and ideas at the workplace. They can think of several unique and out-of-the-box ideas, and they take pleasure in being able to share it and see it implemented in some way. Not getting involved in this manner makes them feel stifled and somewhat suffocated.

2) Enlist the support of others

The Performer Profile must be admired and looked up to. They not only want to excel and be worthwhile and valuable, they want to impress others. It will be good for them to solidify support among their colleagues, and garner support for their ideas. They can reach out to people and sell them on their ideas.

3) Read and gather information

Because who they are, and their ideas, are their source of success, Performer Profiles need to "fill the well," so to speak. They will do well to constantly read and stay updated on latest happenings, innovations, discoveries, and trends, as well as simply gathering knowledge. Different thoughts and ideas will inspire them, and the more they gain external input, the more it will spark them off to create and come up with new ideas and to find alternative or different ways of thinking.

4) Avoid burning out

Performer Profiles are extremely susceptible to burning out. They may push themselves too hard, and not know how to pace themselves. However, there is no use in pushing themselves past the brink and suffering a breakdown as a result. They must learn to how to prioritise, and delegate some of their tasks. Also, it would be good for them to practice self-reflection and ask themselves why they're doing something – for its inherent worth and usefulness, or simply to impress others?

5) Find passion projects

Performer Profiles should ideally work on projects that they're excited about, and think less on what other people are excited about. Naturally, working on something obscure and under-appreciated doesn't appeal to them anyway, but they need to find out where their interest lies – and work in that direction. They should spend less time thinking about what other people find interesting. Finding their own passion projects will help them engage both heart and mind.

6) Take risks

Often times, Performer Profiles are held back from doing something because they're overly concerned about public approval, and doing what's appropriate. However, it's imperative for them to learn how to take small risks and go out on a limb. Not everything has to be a success, and not everything leads to measurable results. They should take a chance on projects that may not go anywhere, but can teach them invaluable skills.

7) Experience more

Similar to reading and gathering information Performer Profiles need to be experience more of life – a plethora of life experiences is fuel for their fire. Travel, meeting new people, seeing new places and things, tasting new food, listening to new music – all of this goes towards building a treasure trove of valuable experiences which the Performer Profile can dip into anytime for creative ideas or inspiration.

8) Brand themselves

Performer Profiles should realise that they are their own product. Therefore, it's extremely important for them to invest in themselves and cultivate their personal brand. This means improving themselves intellectually, mentally, emotionally, and physically – developing new skills and talents and capabilities that will only serve to enrich "their brand".

靈感
Inspiration

The Performer Profile Leadership Style

The People-oriented Leader

The People-oriented style of leadership is somewhat opposite of the task-oriented leadership. Here, the Performer Profile leader is focused on organising, supporting, and developing the people in the team, group, or department. It is a participative style in that it tends to lead to good teamwork and collaboration, but there is also a centre-figure – the Performer Profile leader – who provides the inspiration and is the point of gravity that drums up support, excitement, and sets the big-picture objective.

IDEAL in situations where all the team members are skilful and eager to display creative input; and where the final objective depends entirely on consistent team-work and collective agreement. Creative, loose-flowing projects that depend a lot on brainstorming and self-expression will benefit best

under this form of leadership. LESS IDEAL in situations that require one-on-one work, or periods of solitary work that may benefit from occasional separation between group members. It is less effective when there are many detailed, technical tasks that require close monitoring at the individual stages. It also will not work to best effect in a group with a low sense of camaraderie and trust among members or peers.

Further traits displayed by the Philosopher Profile leader at work:

Inspiring others

The Performer Profile leader is one who aims to inspire others to take action and strive towards objectives. They do this through their speech and words, and the way they articulately and expressively project their ideas, goals, and concepts. They tend to brand themselves through how they express their philosophy of life and work, and through their articulacy are able to artfully influence and inspire the people whom they're leading or working with. They will cheer others on and desire to be looked up to and admired for this.

Persuasive and influential

Performer Profile leaders are usually very good at influencing others and making a dent on the way others think. They are adept at painting vivid and intellectually-resonant pictures, and with their enthusiasm and sense of articulate speech, can win over their subordinates or team-members and drum up and gain a tremendous sense of support for what they're doing.

Creates group identity

Just as they are skilled at branding themselves, Performance Profile leaders are good at crafting a group or team identity. They will build an image for their particular team or department as being the best or the most exclusive, and will firmly extend their own personal self-image to merge with this group. In this sense, they will win over their subordinates who will respect this kind of involvement.

Branding

Along with carving out a strong sense of group identity, Performer Profiles will also brand themselves and the team. They will create a strong story; a narrative that others can believe in and invest in. They will come up with the target and the focus, and round up the excitement needed to ensure group success.

品牌
Branding

Identifying the Super Performer Profile at Work: The Workaholic

When their qualities are manifested in excess, there is something known as the Super Performer Profile – in other words, The Workaholic. These are some of their basic traits, and the ways in which to best respond to them:

- The Workaholic, as the name suggests, cares too much about reaching to the final ground and too little about what they need to do to get there. As such, they can be especially prone to overworking themselves, and their immediate colleagues and subordinates. They find themselves unable to stop working. Others should help them disengage by being quite insistent that they slow down, and harnessing group consensus. The Super Performer Profile does not like to be disliked or disapproved of in a group, and will reconsider.

• The Workaholic has difficulty expressing feelings and engaging with his deepest needs and wants. As such, they may only be operating on a surface or shallow level that is almost robotic, where they keep churning out results and more results. They tend to express affection through the accomplishment of things for their partner and by meeting practical expectations. Partners and close friends will do well to try to engage The Workaholic in more solitary, heart-to-heart chats to enable them to express their feelings. They are expressive, and have the means of doing so – but it's just that they've repressed it under non-stop working habits.

• Workaholics may start to see all their relationships (both personal and professional) in terms of functional roles, transactions, and tasks lists, and by determining how well they and the people in their lives are fulfilling these roles. They need to be reminded every so often that they're doing this, and that they're pushing people away. The Performer Profile relates to words, and therefore speaking to them consistently and repeatedly about the same issue will help them see things in perspective.

• The Workaholics can become quite confused with their own personal goals and the goals of the company or team at large. They care too much about their own agenda, and may start to neglect the bigger picture. It will be important for them to learn how to fuse their personal goals with professional goals, or else they may find themselves going out on a limb and being relegated to the sidelines. In some very extreme or dramatic cases, they may even be liable to losing their position.

工作狂

Workaholics

Famous Performer Profiles

- **Angela Merkel**

Angela Merkel is the current Chancellor of Germany, and is the country's first female Chancellor. Between the years 2006 to 2009, Forbes magazine has listed her as one of the most powerful women in the world.

• Tiger Woods

Tiger Woods is an American professional golfer and a sporting superstar. Currently, he is ranked the World #1 in golf. He is also heavily involved in many charitable activities, chiefly through one of his foundations, The Tiger Woods Foundation. Woods is as much famous for his golf skills as he is for his personality – a Performer Profile who has forged a brand out of both expertise and presentation. His creative sense of play gave golf a new image, and he magnifies attraction and creates a unique identity with his expressive demeanour. Typical of Performer Profiles, as well, he is not without controversy.

• Gordon Ramsay

Gordon Ramsay is a British superstar chef, TV personality, and restaurateur. He is best known for his TV shows Hell's Kitchen, The F Word and Ramsay's Kitchen Nightmares. His personal brand of "ferocious bad-tempered cook" is the fact that has made him as famous as he is. Loud, brash, and utterly unforgettable – Ramsay is the perfect embodiment of the Performer Profile where Ramsay the brand and Ramsay the person do not disconnect. Fantastic showmanship skills combined with expertise and assiduous sense of perfection – along with vibrant energy – makes him a star chef that others can't look away from.

Dealing With The Performer Profile

These are some suggestions for how to deal with the Performer Profile person in your life – whether in a professional or personal capacity:

- **Give them space**

When Performer Profiles are working, they need to be left alone and cannot be disturbed – unless of course it's a brainstorming session and they're actively seeking comments! Then they get annoyed with non-responsiveness. But generally, when they're knuckling down and getting to the heart of things, they cannot be stifled or be harassed.

- **Don't burden them with worries**

For the most part, Performer Profiles cannot be burdened with other people's anxieties. They love giving advice and tips, but they cannot handle others' real emotional problems, issues or worries. They will become flustered, because those problems interfere with their goals and objectives, and they may become curt and or plain rude. Save yourself the trouble and don't even go there.

• **Flatter them**

They love to be adored, so flatter the Performer Profiles by telling them how much you like them, and how much you appreciate them. Let them know that you enjoy being around them, and that you do indeed find them to be very special and one-of-a-kind. They thrive under effusive compliments, and despite appearing "modest" (or trying to), they can never get too much of it.

- **Give criticism with a dose of honey**

Performer Profiles are too fragile to handle raw, unvarnished criticism and feedback of their stuff. They do appreciate the honesty, and do need to know exactly what others think – but how the criticism is presented to them is very important. Sugar-coating it and hiding the critical response amidst other praise will do very well for the Performer Profile; their ego will not suffer a massive wallop.

- **Be proud of their accomplishments**

When the Performer Profile has accomplished something or achieved some success, they cannot handle a "Ho-hum" response. In fact, try not to even yawn. It will cut them to the quick, and shatter their good spirits and sense of self. It will be important to tell them that they have earned some pride, and deserve to be happy.

• **Don't upstage them**

In most cases, let the Performer Profile have centre stage – unless you're another Performer Profile, in which case... let the competitions begin! However, in general, for other people who don't need the limelight as much, let the Performer Profile take the spotlight – especially on particular events or parties where they are meant to take centre-stage.

Paths to Growth for the Performer Profile

Personal Growth Recommendations

Performer Profiles can take certain steps and measures for personal growth; to ensure that they bring out their strengths and learn to manage their weaknesses. Here are some suggestions:

Respect their own emotions

Performer Profiles must learn to accept their own emotions, even if it may be unpleasant. They need to be truthful, and be honest with themselves and with others about their genuine feelings and needs. They should resist the temptation to put on a brave or glamorous front or facade all the time – it is not needed, and not everyone is watching their every move. It's important to get in touch with authentic feelings.

Cooperate with people

Performer Profiles should learn to develop charity and cooperation in all their relationships with other people. It's a matter of simply taking time out from a busy day to catch up with people they care about, or letting someone else win something for a change. They need to compare less, and not always be in an eternal battle for the biggest prize with everyone else.

Pause while working

Taking a breather or a moment to stop and reflect, while in the midst of a busy schedule, is not an act of weakness – it's an act of sanity. There is no need to be a human automaton, efficiently pumping out work and results despite fatigue or depression. It will be important in the long run to learn to take breaks, so as not to exhaust themselves and others.

Care less about reputation

Performer Profiles should learn to care less about their reputation and image, and more on the fundamentals – their personal attitudes, their principles and values in life, and the hows and whys they go about achieving things. Their perception should include less externals – public acclaim, for instance – and more on their own self-satisfaction, contentment, and happiness.

Develop social awareness

It will be especially significant for Performer Profiles to hone and sharpen their social awareness, and get involved in important and charitable causes outside of the self. They need to get outside of their own little universe, and find ways to work with others towards goals that transcend personal interest. This will help the Performer Profile person get in touch with the power of their true value and identity.

Set the bar of success

The best way to live a life less complicated and wrecked by doubt is for the Performer Profile to set the bar of success on their own terms. This means no wondering about what the cool people do, or how to beat so-so at the game, or what move to make in order to be admired. It just means defining success by what they think is important, and working towards those meaningful goals.

Stay focused

Performer Profiles often have numerous wide-ranging interests, and this can be a good thing, but becomes ineffective if they allow themselves to be spread out too thin. Or in the cases of some unhealthy Performer Profiles, they become a dilettante and a dabbler – a Jack of all trades but master of none. It will be important for them to therefore concentrate on their core passions and develop it to success. Find what makes them tick the most, and work on making

that their areas of development. They should be discerning in what they choose to focus their energies on. It is the same with relationships – Performer Profiles cultivate so many that they tend to focus on the upsets of heartbreak, or separation, or parting. Instead, they should work hard at the relationships that mean the most to them, and focus on creating happiness in those.

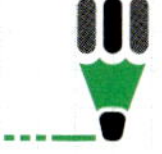

WHAT'S NEXT FOR ME?
– Simple –
Be a Better YOU!

Now that you've read the books and understood what you can do to better yourself, there are other avenues to explore in your journey towards full self-improvement.

Delve deeper into BaZi Profiling with any one of these options:

1) Get a full BaZi Profiling™ Report:

Get a full report personalised to your Day Master, Structure, and Profile. Find out more about the other aspects of your unique personality profile and take massive action to improve your life! The first step to positive *Change*, is *Awareness*. The purpose of the BaZi Profiling™ Report is to help you be AWARE of your full scope of strengths, weaknesses, obvious and hidden talents, positive and negative nature.

www.baziprofiling.com

2) Get BaZi Profiling™ Coaching:

Let us help YOU be a BETTER YOU. Let us help you interpret your BaZi Profile™. You want an unbias and clear view of your chart? No problem - Just call us. Let us coach you based on your BaZi Profile to set achievable goals, create better business systems, improve work performance and rectify relationship setbacks. Meet our Bazi Profiling™ coaches to book a one-on-one session and set you sailing on your path of least resistence to success and happiness. We will help you be, a Better You.

Tel: +6(03) 2284 8080

Email: profile@masteryacademy.com

3) Join Joey Yap's "Design Your Destiny" workshop:

Top leaders of the world will tell you – PEOPLE knowledge, is more important than product knowledge. Successful entreprenuers will tell you it's the ability to work with PEOPLE is what separates successes from failures. Sit down with teachers, small business owners, traders, professionals and parents – they will tell you that PEOPLE knowledge make the difference between those who excel and those who don't.

All of life's successes come from initiating the right connections with the right people and then strengthening and building those connections by PEOPLE Knowledge.

To understand and learn about PEOPLE (and yourself)– attend a **Design Your Destiny** workshop. It's a workshop based entirely on Joey Yap's "BaZi Profilling™ System. You will learn all about the different BaZi Profiles and more importantly - HOW to motivate, inspire, change, help and persuade them positively. Help others (and yourself) be BETTER.

www.masteryacademy.com/DYD

About Joey Yap

Joey Yap is the founder of the Mastery Academy of Chinese Metaphysics, a global organization devoted to the teaching of Feng Shui, BaZi, Mian Xiang and other Chinese Metaphysics subjects. He is also the Chief Consultant of Yap Global Consulting, an international consulting firm specialising in Feng Shui and Chinese Astrology services and audits.

Joey Yap is the bestselling author of over 30 books on Feng Shui, Chinese Astrology, Face Reading and Yi Jing, many of which have topped the Malaysian and Singaporean MPH bookstores' bestseller lists.

Thousands of students from all around the world have learnt and mastered Classical Feng Shui, Chinese Astrology, and other Chinese Metaphysics subjects through Joey Yap's structured learning programs, books and online training. Joey Yap's courses are currently taught by over 30 instructors worldwide.

Every year Joey Yap conducts his 'Feng Shui and Astrology' seminar to a crowd of more than 3500 people at the Kuala Lumpur Convention Center. He also takes this annual seminar on a world tour to Frankfurt, San Francisco, New York, Toronto, London, Sydney and Singapore.

In addition to being a regular guest on various radio and TV shows, Joey Yap has also written columns for The New Straits Times and The Star - Malaysia's two leading newspapers. He has also been featured in many popular global publications and networks like Time International, Forbes International, the International Herald Tribune and Bloomberg.

He has also hosted his own TV series, 'Discover Feng Shui with Joey Yap', on 8TV, a local Malaysian network in 2005; and 'Walking The Dragons with Joey Yap' on Astro Wah Lai Toi, Malaysia's cable network in 2008.

Joey Yap has worked with HSBC, Bloomberg, Microsoft, Samsung, IBM, HP, Alliance, Great Eastern, Citibank, Standard Chartered, OCBC, SIME UEP, Mah Sing, Auto Bavaria, Volvo, AXA, Singtel, ABN Amro, CIMB, Hong-Leong, Manulife and others.

Author's personal website :www.joeyyap.com

Follow Joey Yap's regular updates on Twitter:

www.twitter.com/joeyyap

Joey Yap on Facebook:

www.facebook.com/JoeyYapFB

EDUCATION

The Mastery Academy of Chinese Metaphysics: the first choice for practitioners and aspiring students of the art and science of Chinese Classical Feng Shui and Astrology.

For thousands of years, Eastern knowledge has been passed from one generation to another through the system of discipleship. A venerated master would accept suitable individuals at a young age as his disciples, and informally through the years, pass on his knowledge and skills to them. His disciples in turn, would take on their own disciples, as a means to perpetuate knowledge or skills.

This system served the purpose of restricting the transfer of knowledge to only worthy honourable individuals and ensuring that outsiders or Westerners would not have access to thousands of years of Eastern knowledge, learning and research.

However, the disciple system has also resulted in Chinese Metaphysics and Classical Studies lacking systematic teaching methods. Knowledge garnered over the years has not been accumulated in a concise, systematic manner, but scattered amongst practitioners, each practicing his/her knowledge, art and science, in isolation.

The disciple system, out of place in today's modern world, endangers the advancement of these classical fields that continue to have great relevance and application today.

At the Mastery Academy of Chinese Metaphysics, our Mission is to bring Eastern Classical knowledge in the fields of metaphysics, Feng Shui and Astrology sciences and the arts to the world. These Classical teachings and knowledge, previously shrouded in secrecy and passed on only through the discipleship system, are adapted into structured learning, which can easily be understood, learnt and mastered. Through modern learning methods, these renowned ancient arts, sciences and practices can be perpetuated while facilitating more extensive application and understanding of these classical subjects.

The Mastery Academy espouses an educational philosophy that draws from the best of the East and West. It is the world's premier educational institution for the study of Chinese Metaphysics Studies offering a wide range and variety of courses, ensuring that students have the opportunity to pursue their preferred field of study and enabling existing practitioners and professionals to gain cross-disciplinary knowledge that complements their current field of practice.

Courses at the Mastery Academy have been carefully designed to ensure a comprehensive yet compact syllabus. The modular nature of the courses enables students to immediately begin to put their knowledge into practice while pursuing continued study of their field and complementary fields. Students thus have the benefit of developing and gaining practical experience in tandem with the expansion and advancement of their theoretical knowledge.

Students can also choose from a variety of study options, from a distance learning program, the Homestudy Series, that enables study at one's own pace or intensive foundation courses and compact lecture-based courses, held in various cities around the world by Joey Yap or our licensed instructors. The Mastery Academy's faculty and make-up is international in nature, thus ensuring that prospective students can attend courses at destinations nearest to their country of origin or with a licensed Mastery Academy instructor in their home country.

The Mastery Academy provides 24x7 support to students through its Online Community, with a variety of tools, documents, forums and e-learning materials to help students stay at the forefront of research in their fields and gain invaluable assistance from peers and mentoring from their instructors.

MASTERY ACADEMY
OF CHINESE METAPHYSICS

www.masteryacademy.com

MALAYSIA

19-3, The Boulevard, Mid Valley City, 59200 Kuala Lumpur, Malaysia
Tel : +603-2284 8080 Fax : +603-2284 1218 Email : info@masteryacademy.com

Australia, Austria, Canada, China, Croatia, Cyprus, Czech Republic, Denmark, France, Germany, Greece, Hungary, India, Italy, Kazakhstan, Malaysia, Netherlands (Holland), New Zealand, Philippines, Poland, Russian Federation, Singapore, Slovenia, South Africa, Switzerland, Turkey, U.S.A., Ukraine, United Kingdom

Mastery Academy around the world

Feng Shui Consultations

For Residential Properties
- Initial Land/Property Assessment
- Residential Feng Shui Consultations
- Residential Land Selection
- End-to-End Residential Consultation

For Commercial Properties
- Initial Land/Property Assessment
- Commercial Feng Shui Consultations
- Commercial Land Selection
- End-to-End Commercial Consultation

For Property Developers
- End-to-End Consultation
- Post-Consultation Advisory Services
- Panel Feng Shui Consultant

For Property Investors
- Your Personal Feng Shui Consultant
- Tailor-Made Packages

For Memorial Parks & Burial Sites
- Yin House Feng Shui

BaZi Consultations

Personal Destiny Analysis
- Personal Destiny Analysis for Individuals
- Children's BaZi Analysis
- Family BaZi Analysis

Strategic Analysis for Corporate Organizations
- Corporate BaZi Consultations
- BaZi Analysis for Human Resource Management

Entrepreneurs & Business Owners
- BaZi Analysis for Entrepreneurs

Career Pursuits
- BaZi Career Analysis

Relationships
- Marriage and Compatibility Analysis
- Partnership Analysis

For Everyone
- Annual BaZi Forecast
- Your Personal BaZi Coach

Date Selection Consultations

- **Marriage Date Selection**
- **Caesarean Birth Date Selection**
- **House-Moving Date Selection**
- **Renovation & Groundbreaking Dates**
- **Signing of Contracts**
- **Official Openings**
- **Product Launches**

Yi Jing Assessment

A Time-Tested, Accurate Science

• With a history predating 4 millennia, the Yi Jing - or Classic of Change - is one of the oldest Chinese texts surviving today. Its purpose as an oracle, in predicting the outcome of things, is based on the variables of Time, Space and Specific Events.

• A Yi Jing Assessment provides specific answers to any specific questions you may have about a specific event or endeavor. This is something that a Destiny Analysis would not be able to give you.

Basically, what a Yi Jing Assessment does is focus on only ONE aspect or item at a particular point in your life, and give you a calculated prediction of the details that will follow suit, if you undertake a particular action. It gives you an insight into a situation, and what course of action to take in order to arrive at a satisfactory outcome at the end of the day.

Please Contact YGC for a personalized Yi Jing Assessment!

Tel: +603-2284 1213 Email: consultation@joeyyap.com

Chinese Metaphysics Reference Series

The Chinese Metaphysics Reference Series is a collection of reference texts, source material, and educational textbooks to be used as supplementary guides by scholars, students, researchers, teachers and practitioners of Chinese Metaphysics.

These comprehensive and structured books provide fast, easy reference to aid in the study and practice of various Chinese Metaphysics subjects including Feng Shui, BaZi, Yi Jing, Zi Wei, Liu Ren, Ze Ri, Ta Yi, Qi Men and Mian Xiang.

The Ten Thousand Year Calendar

The Chinese Metaphysics Compendium

Dong Gong Date Selection

The Date Selection Compendium

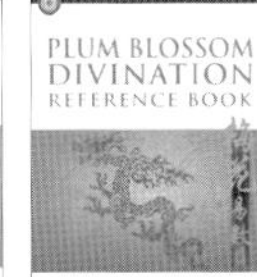

Plum Blossoms Divination Reference Book

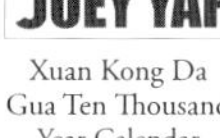

Xuan Kong Da Gua Ten Thousand Year Calendar

Xuan Kong Da Gua Structures Reference Book

Xuan Kong Da Gua 64 Gua Transformation Analysis

Xuan Kong Purple White Script

Earth Study Discern Truth Second Edition

Bazi Structures and Structural Useful Gods - Wood

Bazi Structures and Structural Useful Gods - Fire

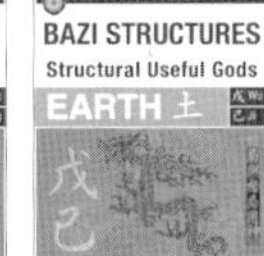

Bazi Structures and Structural Useful Gods - Earth

Bazi Structures and Structural Useful Gods - Metal

Bazi Structures and Structural Useful Gods - Water

Books: Feng Shui for Homebuyers Series

Feng Shui For Homebuyers - Exterior
(English & Chinese versions)

Feng Shui for Homebuyers - Interior
(English & Chinese versions)

Feng Shui for Apartment Buyers - Home Owners

Books: Stories and Lessons on Feng Shui Series

Stories and Lessons on Feng Shui
(English & Chinese versions)

More Stories and Lessons on Feng Shui

Even More Stories and Lessons on Feng Shui

Continue Your Journey with Joey Yap's Books

Walking the Dragons

Your Aquarium Here

The Art of Date Selection: Personal Date Selection

Xuan Kong Flying Stars Feng Shui

Pure Feng Shui

Books: BaZi - The Destiny Code Series

BaZi - The Destiny Code (English & Chinese versions)

BaZi - The Destiny Code Revealed

Meet Your Day Master & Get To Know Yourself!

Find out your Day Master for FREE! **www.joeyyap.com/DM**

(English & Chinese versions)

The BaZi Essentials series of books comprise 10 individual books that focus on the individual Day Masters in BaZi (Four Pillars of Destiny, or Chinese Astrology) study and analysis. With each book focusing on one particular Day Master, Joey explains why the Day Master is the fundamental starting point for BaZi analysis, and is the true essence of one's character traits and basic identity.

With these concise and entertaining books that are designed to be both informative and entertaining, Joey shows how each person is different and unique, yet share similar traits, according to his or her respective Day Master. These 10 guides will provide crucial insight into why people behave in the various different ways they do.

Get to know your BaZi Structure... and Understand How You Approach the World

Find out your Profile for FREE! **www.joeyyap.com/profile**

Joey Yap's BaZi Structures series of books comprises 5 individual titles to help you interact with the world.

While your Day Master shows you who you are, your Structure tells you about your behaviour and attitude in relation to the world. In this series, your strengths and weaknesses in how you relate to people and events in terms of work, family, and friendship all come to the fore. Each book in this series concentrates on one specific Structure, and provides clues on ideal careers, job roles, and wealth paths for that Structure.

Furthermore, these 5 guides will provide the blueprint to knowing why some people are the way they are, and what to do to help you deal with the varied and colourful characters in your life.

Books: Face Reading Series

Mian Xiang - Discover Face Reading (English & Chinese versions)

Joey Yap's Art of Face Reading

Easy Guide on Face Reading

All you need to know about the Eyes, Eyebrows, Mouth, Nose and Ears.

Joey Yap's brand new Face Reading Essentials Series are easy, fast, and effective guides for beginners, enthusiasts, and the curious. Learn to read your face by identifying the facial features on your own face, and the faces of the people around you.

These are EASY, FAST and EFFECTIVE guides for beginners, enthusiasts, and the curious. Make first impressions work for you by applying Face Reading skills to understand the personality and character of the person standing in front of you, whether at work, in business meetings, on a date, or anywhere else!

(English & Chinese versions)

Annual Releases

Chinese Astrology for 2011

Feng Shui for 2011

Tong Shu Diary 2011

Weekly Tong Shu Diary 2011

Tong Shu Monthly Planner 2010

Professional Tong Shu Diary 2011

Tong Shu Desktop Calendar 2011

Educational Tools & Software

Xuan Kong Flying Stars Feng Shui Software

The Essential Application for Enthusiasts and Professionals

Highlights of the software include:

- Natal Flying Stars
- Monthly Flying Stars
- 81 Flying Stars Combinations
- Dual-View Format
- Annual Flying Stars
- Flying Stars Integration
- 24 Mountains

All charts will be are printable and configurable, and can be saved for future editing. Also, you'll be able to export your charts into most image file formats like jpeg, bmp, and gif.

Mini Feng Shui Compass

The Mini Feng Shui Compass is a self-aligning compass that is not only light at 100gms but also built sturdily to ensure it will be convenient to use anywhere. The rings on the Mini Feng Shui Compass are bi-lingual and incorporate the 24 Mountain Rings that is used in your traditional Luo Pan.

BaZi Ming Pan Software Version 2.0

Professional Four Pillars Calculator for Destiny Analysis

The BaZi Ming Pan Version 2.0 Professional Four Pillars Calculator for Destiny Analysis is the most technically advanced software of its kind in the world today. It allows even those without any knowledge of BaZi to generate their own BaZi Charts, and provides virtually every detail required to undertake a comprehensive Destiny Analysis.

Joey Yap Feng Shui Template Set

The Set comprises 3 basic templates: The Basic Feng Shui Template, 8 Mansions Feng Shui Template, and the Flying Stars Feng Shui Template.

Main Features:

- Easy-to-use, simple, and straightforward
- Small and portable; each template measuring only 5" x 5"
- Additional 8 Mansions and Flying Stars Reference Rings
- Handy companion booklet with usage tips and examples

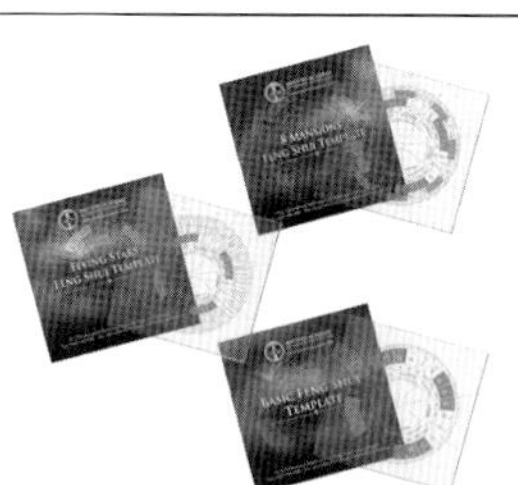

Feng Shui for Homebuyers DVD Series

In these DVDs, Joey will guide you on how to customise your home to maximise the Feng Shui potential of your property and gain the full benefit of improving your health, wealth and love life using the 9 Palace Grid. He will show you how to go about applying the classical applications of the Life Gua and House Gua techniques to get attuned to your Sheng Qi (positive energies).

Accelerate Your Face Reading Skills With Joey Yap's Face Reading Revealed DVD Series

In these highly entertaining DVDs, Joey will help you answer all these questions and more. You will be able to ascertain the underlying meaning of moles, birthmarks or even the type of your hair in Face Reading. Joey will also reveal the guidelines to help you foster better and stronger relationships with your loved ones through Mian Xiang.

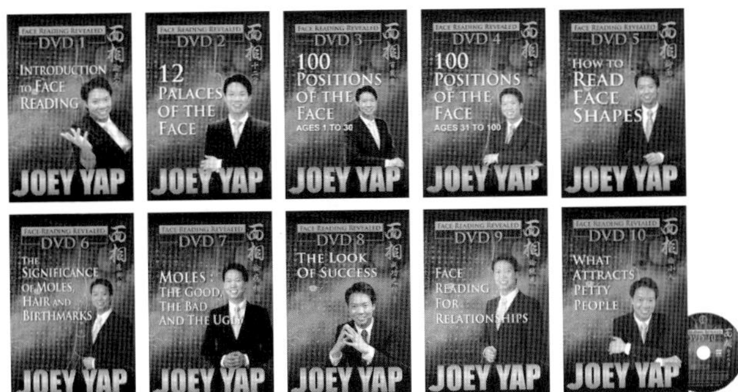

Discover Feng Shui with Joey Yap (TV Series) - Set of 4 DVDS

Discover Feng Shui with Joey Yap: Set of 4 DVDs

Informative and entertaining, classical Feng Shui comes alive in *Discover Feng Shui with Joey Yap!*

Dying to know how you can use Feng Shui to improve your house or office, but simply too busy attend for formal classes?

You have the questions. Now let Joey personally answer them in this 4-set DVD compilation! Learn how to ensure the viability of your residence or workplace, Feng Shui-wise, without having to convert it into a Chinese antiques' shop. Classical Feng Shui is about harnessing the natural power of your environment to improve quality of life. It's a systematic and subtle metaphysical science.

And that's not all. Joey also debunks many a myth about classical Feng Shui, and shares with viewers Face Reading tips as well!

Own the series that national channel 8TV did a re-run of in 2005, today!

Elevate Your Feng Shui Skills With Joey Yap's Home Study Course And Educational DVDs

Xuan Kong Vol.1
An Advanced Feng Shui Home Study Course

Feng Shui for Period 8 - (DVD)

Xuan Kong Flying Stars Beginners Workshop - (DVD)

BaZi Four Pillars of Destiny Beginners Workshop - (DVD)

Interested in learning MORE about Feng Shui? Advance Your Feng Shui Knowledge with the Mastery Academy Courses.

Feng Shui Mastery Series™
LIVE COURSES (MODULES ONE TO FOUR)

The Feng Shui Mastery Series comprises Feng Shui Mastery Modules 1, 2, 3, and 4. It is a program that introduces students to the theories, principles, analyses, and interpretations of classical Feng Shui. It is a thorough, comprehensive program that covers important theories from various classical Feng Shui systems including Ba Zhai, San Yuan, San He, and Xuan Kong.

BaZi Mastery Series™
LIVE COURSES (MODULES ONE TO FOUR)

The BaZi Mastery Series comprises BaZi Mastery Modules 1, 2, 3, and 4 which provides students with a thorough introduction to BaZi, along with an intensive understanding of BaZi principles and the requisite skills to practice it with accuracy and precision. Students who complete these modules will be well-prepared to perform readings and interpretations. Feng Shui practitioners will also benefit from having knowledge of BaZi, as it will complement and enhance their Feng Shui practice.

www.masteryacademy.com

Xuan Kong Mastery Series™

LIVE COURSES (MODULES ONE TO THREE)

* Advanced Courses For Master Practitioners

The Xuan Kong Mastery Series allows students to take their introductory steps into the captivating world of this powerful science. While Classical Feng Shui is always about the study of Location and Direction, Xuan Kong factors in the concept of Time into the equation as well. This course that will expose students to the extremely advanced techniques and formulas based upon those that were used by the ancient masters, as derived from the classics.It paves the way for students to specialize in the intelligent and strategic allocation of Qi, allowing them to literally manipulate Qi to assist in their life endeavours.

Mian Xiang Mastery Series™

LIVE COURSES (MODULES ONE AND TWO)

As one of the time-tested Five Arts (Wu Xing) of Chinese Metaphysics, Mian Xiang falls under the study of the physiognomy of the features, contours, shapes and hues of the face. In Mian Xiang, however, a person's face is more than what he or she shows the world; it's also a virtual map of this person's potential and destiny in life.

The Mian Xiang Mastery Series comprises Module 1 and Module 2 to allow students to learn this ancient art in a thorough, detailed manner. Each module has a carefully-developed syllabus that allows students to get acquainted with the fundamentals of Mian Xiang before moving on to the more intricate theories and principles that will enable them to practice Mian Xiang with greater depth and complexity.

+603 - 2284 8080

Yi Jing Mastery Series™

LIVE COURSES (MODULES ONE AND TWO)

'Yi' relates to change. Indeed, flux - or continuous change - is the key concept of the Yi Jing. Change is the only constant in life, and there is no exception to this rule. Evolution, transformation, alteration - call it by any other name, its effects are still far-reaching and encompasses every law - natural or manmade - known to our universe.

The Yi Jing Mastery Series provides an introductory look into the basics and fundamentals of Yi Jing thought and theory. As the Yi Jing functioned as an ancient Chinese oracle thousands of years ago, this Module will explore Yi Jing as a science of divination and probe the ways in which the concept of 'change' plays a big part in Yi Jing. Together both modules aim to give casual and serious Yi Jing enthusiasts a serious insight into one of the most important philosophical treatises in ancient Chinese thought.

Ze Ri Mastery Series™

LIVE COURSES (MODULES ONE AND TWO)

The ZeRi Mastery Series, or Date Selection, comprise two modules: ZeRi Mastery Series Module 1 and ZeRi Mastery Series Module 2. This program provides students with a thorough introduction to the art of Date Selection both for Personal and Feng Shui purposes. Both modules provide a fundamental grounding in all the rudimentary basics and allow you to move from the more straightforward techniques in Module 1 to the more sophisticated methods of Xuan Kong Da Gua in Module 2 with ease and confidence.

Feng Shui for Life

Feng Shui for life is a 5-day course designed for the Feng Shui beginner to learn how to apply practical Feng Shui in day-to-day living. It is a culmination of powerful tools and techniques that allows you to gain quick proficiency in Classical Feng Shui.

Mastery Academy courses are conducted around the world. Find out when will Joey Yap be in your area by visiting **www.masteryacademy.com** or call our office at **+603-2284 8080**.